D1462189

starters

Rick Stein *starters*

Published by BBC Books, BBC Worldwide Ltd,
Woodlands, 80 Wood Lane, London W12 0TT

First published 2004
4 6 8 10 9 7 5
Copyright © Rick Stein 2004
The moral right of the author has been asserted

Food photography © Laurie Evans 1997 and
James Murphy 1999, 2000, 2002 and 2004
Portrait of Rick Stein and Chalky on page 6
© David Pritchard 1999

The recipes in this book first appeared in the
following titles: **Fruits of the Sea**, **Seafood Odyssey**,
Seafood Lovers' Guide, **Seafood**, **Food Heroes** and
Food Heroes: Another Helping, which were
originally published by BBC Worldwide in 1997,
1999, 2000, 2001, 2002 and 2004 respectively.

ISBN 978 0 563 52189 1

Commissioning Editor: Vivien Bowler
Project Editors: Rachel Copus and Warren Albers
Designer: Andrew Barron
Production Controller: Kenneth McKay
Food Stylist: Debbie Major

Set in Din and Veljovic
Printed and bound in Singapore
Colour separations by Butler and Tanner Ltd

Jacket photography:
Food photography and portrait of Rick Stein
© James Murphy 2004
Landscape photography © Craig Easton 2000

contents

There's a lot to read in most cookery books. Sometimes I think one is spoiled for choice. Guided by the theory that 'less is more', I thought that three books each containing a dozen or so recipes covering first courses, main courses and puddings would be a welcome alternative. So I've compiled three mini cookery books, choosing the recipes from the nine books I've written to give the widest possible range of dishes that best illustrate my personal style of cooking. I like to think of them as my 'best of' recipe collections.

To illustrate this, I joke with the producer of my TV series, David Pritchard, that most of his CD collection seems to be labelled 'The best of'. I call him Compilation Man, which hurts him a little because actually he has a very acute knowledge of music. But sometimes a slim volume of 'best of' dishes like this sets a boundary on cooking at a time when you might be suffering from information overload.

I have fanciful thoughts that these would be all you need, say, on holiday, cooking in a rented house or villa. You could slip these slim volumes into your luggage and be armed with a repertoire of enough dishes to deal with a light lunch over a glass of wine, supper for the children or a serious dinner for a party of friends.

Most of these first courses could serve as main courses, light lunches or supper dishes as well. **Cod and lobster chowder** could, after all, be classed as a fish soup or a stew. I love that subtle combination of salt pork, seafood and cream. The recipe is really special, made with lobster – but not a great deal – and the soft parts are used to thicken the soup.

You could make **Mouclade** too into a much larger main course. One of my most loved dishes, mussels with a creamy sauce flavoured with a pinch of curry powder and saffron, it originated in the Charente-Maritime in France where local mussels were married to spice landed from boats coming from the East Indies.

Understandably, I've included a predominance of seafood in my first courses, dishes like **Gremolata prawns**, a recipe to use when you have some first-class prawns in the shell. You just stir-fry them in olive oil, then sprinkle with parsley, lemon zest and garlic and eat them with your fingers. **Stir-fried salt and pepper squid** is another recipe for some top-quality seafood. Don't attempt this unless you've got the best squid: firm and not running wet, with a lustrous brown-white skin, no signs of a mauve tinge and no smell.

The search for perfectly fresh seafood is often difficult but not impossible. You'll certainly need some good scallops, preferably still in the shell, for **Grilled scallops in the shell**. **Sautéed red mullet with spaghettini** will need some small firm red mullet in glorious hues of pink and yellow. I don't know of many classic Italian fish and pasta dishes, but this is one of them. It comes from Liguria and depends for its success on the seductive combination of fresh fish, fried in olive oil, with pasta, parsley and garlic plus a little chilli and tomato. You fry the fillets skin-on, because there's so much flavour in the skin of red mullet, but the dish works very well with other slightly oily fish, such as sea bream, snapper or small sea bass.

Of late I've been writing cookery books with recipes for meat and poultry and eggs and game, so I've included some of my favourite non-fish dishes, such as **Cured duck breasts with melon**. I first ate this in the 1980s at the legendary restaurant Berowra Waters Inn, on the Hawkesbury River, north of Sydney. You could only get to the restaurant by boat or seaplane from Rose Bay or Palm Beach – so even the arrival was memorable – and this combination of salt duck, sweet melon, pickled ginger and soy is a perfect example of modern Australian cookery. It is so good that I chose it as my first course for the Queen when I cooked dinner at 10 Downing Street during the Golden Jubilee year of 2002. I'm pretty sure it went down well; I didn't get to hear, but nothing came back to the kitchen.

I'm particularly fond of my **Salad of poached eggs with bacon**, a version of the classic salade tiède (warm salad), in which I include a poached egg. The yolk, when broken, mixes with the dressing and coats the salad leaves in a pleasing way. I don't want to appear too doctrinaire, but try using just one variety of salad leaf in this. I find those bags of mixed leaves you get everywhere now a bit boring. They've rather taken the surprise out of a salad, particularly as they seem to have been washed so well as to exclude most of their flavour.

I hope you will enjoy all these recipes, yet I think the one that sums up my cooking best is **Grilled tuna salad with guacamole**, a dish which we still have on the restaurant menu and one that I often prepare when cooking far from home. I served this at a dinner in a very atmospheric American inn, The Joseph Ambler near North Wales (just outside Philadelphia), a couple of months ago. I think the chefs were a bit alarmed to see me coating whole tuna loins with coarse salt and black pepper and searing them viciously on a charcoal grill, but the finished dish – thinly sliced tuna blackened on the outside and very underdone in the centre with a guacamole and a dark soy, spring onion and lemon grass dressing – made the guests very happy.

starters

cod and lobster chowder

1 x 450–550 g (1–1¼ lb)
lobster, freshly cooked
4 water biscuits
50 g (2 oz) butter, softened
100 g (4 oz) salt pork or
rindless streaky bacon,
in one piece
1 small onion, finely chopped
15 g (½ oz) plain flour
1.2 litres (2 pints) milk
2 medium potatoes (about
225 g/8 oz), peeled and diced
1 bay leaf
450 g (1 lb) skinned thick
cod fillet
120 ml (4 fl oz) double cream
A pinch of cayenne pepper
2 tablespoons
chopped parsley
Salt and freshly ground
black pepper

1 First remove the meat from the cooked lobster
(see page 38), cutting the meat from the tail section into
thin slices and scraping all the white curd-like material out
of the shells.

2 Put 2 of the water biscuits into a plastic bag and crush
to very fine crumbs by rolling them with a rolling pin.
Then mix with the tomalley, other soft material from the
head and half the butter, or blend everything in a small
food processor.

3 Cut the piece of salt pork or bacon into small dice.
Heat the rest of the butter in a medium-sized pan, add the
pork or bacon and fry over a medium heat until lightly
golden. Add the onion and cook gently until softened. Stir
in the flour and cook for 1 minute. Gradually stir in the milk,
then the potatoes and bay leaf and simmer for 10 minutes or
until the potatoes are just tender. Add the cod and simmer
for 4–5 minutes, then break the fish apart into large flakes
with a wooden spoon.

4 Stir in the water biscuit paste, lobster meat and cream
and simmer for 1 minute. Season with the cayenne pepper,
1 teaspoon of salt and some black pepper. To serve, coarsely
crush the 2 remaining water biscuits and sprinkle them over
the soup with the chopped parsley.

gremolata **prawns**

SERVES 4

1 large lemon
2 tablespoons olive oil
20 unpeeled large
raw prawns
Cayenne pepper (optional)
3 garlic cloves,
very finely chopped
4 tablespoons chopped
flat-leaf parsley
Coarse sea salt and
freshly ground black pepper

1 Peel the zest off the lemon with a potato peeler, pile the pieces up a few at a time and then cut them across into short, thin strips. Heat the oil in a large frying pan. Add the prawns and toss them over a high heat for 4–5 minutes, seasoning them with some cayenne pepper or black pepper and sea salt as you do so.

2 Cut the lemon in half and squeeze the juice from one half over the prawns. Continue to cook until the juice has almost evaporated – the prawns should be quite dry. Take the pan off the heat and leave for about 1 minute to cool very slightly. Then sprinkle over the lemon zest, chopped garlic, parsley and ¼ teaspoon of salt and toss together well. Pile the prawns into a large serving dish and serve with some finger bowls and plenty of napkins.

la mouclade

SERVES 4

A good pinch of saffron
1.75 kg (4 lb) mussels,
cleaned (see page 40)
120 ml (4 fl oz) dry white wine
25 g (1 oz) butter
1 small onion, finely chopped
2 garlic cloves, finely chopped
½ teaspoon good-quality
medium curry powder
2 tablespoons cognac
2 teaspoons plain flour
200 ml (7 fl oz) crème fraîche
3 tablespoons
chopped parsley
Salt and freshly ground
black pepper

1 Put the saffron into a small bowl and moisten it with 1 tablespoon of warm water. Place the mussels and wine in a large pan, cover and cook over a high heat for 3–4 minutes, shaking the pan now and then, until the mussels have opened. Tip them into a colander set over a bowl to catch all the cooking liquor and discard any that haven't opened. Transfer the mussels to a large serving bowl and keep warm.

2 Melt the butter in a pan, add the onion, garlic and curry powder and cook gently without browning for 2–3 minutes. Add the cognac and cook until it has almost all evaporated, then stir in the flour and cook for 1 minute. Gradually stir in the saffron liquid and all but the last tablespoon or two of the mussel cooking liquor, which might contain some grit. Bring the sauce to a simmer and cook for 2–3 minutes. Add the crème fraîche and simmer for a further 3 minutes, until slightly reduced. Season to taste, stir in the parsley and then pour the sauce over the mussels. Stir them together gently and serve with plenty of French bread.

NOTE
A mouclade is a classic French dish from the Charente-Maritime region, faintly flavoured with a little curry spice and saffron.

SERVES 4

**750 g (1½ lb) squid, cleaned
(see page 42)
½ teaspoon black peppercorns
½ teaspoon Sichuan
peppercorns
1 teaspoon sea salt flakes
1–2 tablespoons sunflower oil
1 medium-hot red finger
chilli, thinly sliced (seeds
removed, if you prefer)
3 spring onions, sliced**

FOR THE SALAD

**¼ cucumber, peeled,
halved and seeded
50 g (2 oz) beansprouts
25 g (1 oz) watercress, large
stalks removed
2 teaspoons dark soy sauce
2 teaspoons roasted
sesame oil
¼ teaspoon caster sugar
A pinch of salt**

1 For the salad, cut the cucumber lengthways into short strips. Toss with the beansprouts and watercress and set aside in the fridge until needed. Whisk together the soy sauce, sesame oil, sugar and salt.

2 Cut along one side of each squid pouch and open it out flat. Score the inner side in a diamond pattern with the tip of a small, sharp knife and then cut into 5 cm (2 in) squares. Separate the tentacles if large.

3 Heat a small, heavy-based frying pan over a high heat. Add the black peppercorns and Sichuan peppercorns and dry-roast them for a few seconds, shaking the pan now and then, until they darken slightly and become aromatic. Tip into a mortar and crush coarsely with the pestle, then stir in the sea salt flakes.

4 Heat a wok over a high heat until smoking. Add half the oil and half the squid and stir-fry it for 2 minutes, until lightly coloured. Tip on to a plate, then cook the remaining squid in the same way. Return the first batch of squid to the wok and add 1 teaspoon of the salt and pepper mixture (the rest can be used in other stir-fries). Toss together for about 10 seconds, then add the red chilli and spring onions and toss together very briefly. Divide the squid between 4 serving plates. Toss the salad with the dressing and pile alongside the squid, then serve immediately.

SERVES 4

**16 prepared scallops
in the shell
25 g (1 oz) unsalted butter,
melted
Salt and freshly ground
black pepper**

FOR THE TOASTED
HAZELNUT AND
CORIANDER BUTTER
**20 g (¾ oz) unblanched
hazelnuts
75 g (3 oz) unsalted butter,
softened
7 g (¼ oz) coriander leaves
2 tablespoons flat-leaf
parsley leaves
7 g (¼ oz) roughly
chopped shallot
1 teaspoon fresh lemon juice**

1 For the toasted hazelnut and coriander butter, spread the hazelnuts over a baking tray and toast under the grill for 4–5 minutes, shaking the tray now and then, until they are golden brown. Tip them into a clean tea towel and rub off the skins. Leave to cool, then chop them roughly and tip them into a food processor. Add the softened butter with the coriander, parsley, shallot, lemon juice, a good pinch of salt and some pepper and blend together until well mixed.

2 Preheat the grill to high. Place the scallop shells on a large baking tray (or do them in batches if necessary). Brush the scallops with the melted butter and season with a little salt and pepper, then grill for 1½ minutes. Drop a generous teaspoonful of the hazelnut and coriander butter on to each scallop and return to the grill for 1½ minutes, until cooked through. Serve immediately.

salad of poached eggs with bacon

SERVES 4

2 slices white bread
Sunflower oil, for shallow frying
4 rashers rindless thick-cut bacon, cut across into short, fat strips
1 tablespoon white wine vinegar
1 tablespoon salt
4 medium eggs
The pale green leaves from the centre of
1 frisée (curly endive), washed and dried
25 g (1 oz) wild rocket leaves

FOR THE MUSTARD DRESSING
1 teaspoon Dijon mustard
2 teaspoons white wine vinegar
¼ teaspoon salt
3–4 tablespoons sunflower oil

FOR THE PERSILLADE
2 small garlic cloves
A small handful of flat-leaf parsley leaves

1 Cut the crusts from the slices of bread and cut each slice into 1 cm (½ in) cubes. Shallow fry in 1 cm (½ in) oil until crisp and golden. Drain briefly on kitchen paper.

2 For the mustard dressing, whisk together the mustard, vinegar and salt. Gradually whisk in the oil to make a creamy dressing. For the persillade, chop together the garlic and parsley, leaving it a little bit coarse.

3 Heat a little sunflower oil in a frying pan, add the bacon strips and fry for 2–3 minutes until crisp and golden. Keep warm.

4 Bring a couple of inches of water, the white wine vinegar and salt to a simmer in a large, shallow pan. Break in the eggs and poach for 3 minutes. Lift out with a slotted spoon and drain.

5 Toss the frisée and rocket leaves with a little of the mustard dressing and spread over 4 plates. Put a poached egg into the centre of the leaves and scatter over the bacon. Sprinkle with some of the persillade, drizzle over a little more dressing and then scatter over the croûtons. Serve immediately.

cured duck breasts with melon

½ teaspoon black peppercorns
½ teaspoon coriander seeds
1 tablespoon thyme leaves
2 bay leaves
Salt
40 g (1½ oz) sugar
2 large duck breasts
½ Charentais melon, to serve

FOR THE PICKLED GINGER
75 g (3 oz) fresh ginger
1 medium-hot red Dutch chilli,
seeded and thinly sliced
25 g (1 oz) sugar
200 ml (7 fl oz) white
wine vinegar
6 allspice berries
2.5 cm (1 in) cinnamon stick

FOR THE SOY SAUCE
DRESSING
2 teaspoons red wine vinegar
2 teaspoons dark soy sauce
3 tablespoons groundnut oil
A pinch of Sichuan
peppercorns, crushed

1 Grind the peppercorns, coriander seeds, thyme leaves, bay leaves and salt to a fine powder and mix with the sugar. Sprinkle half into a dish and lay the duck breasts, flesh-side down, on top. Cover with the remainder and chill for at least 12 hours.

2 For the pickled ginger, peel the ginger and cut it into fine matchsticks. Mix with the chillies and 1 teaspoon of salt and transfer to a small bowl. Put the rest of the ingredients into a small pan, bring to the boil and simmer for 5 minutes. Pour over the ginger, leave to cool, then cover and leave for at least 24 hours.

3 Preheat the oven to 160°C/325°F/Gas Mark 3. Rinse the salt cure off the duck breasts, put them into a small casserole and add 300 ml (10 fl oz) of water. Cover and cook for 25 minutes. Lift them on to a plate and leave to cool.

4 Just before serving, whisk together the ingredients for the soy sauce dressing. Remove the seeds from the melon with a spoon and cut it into 4 wedges. Slice the flesh neatly away from the skin and then cut it diagonally into thin slices. Slice the duck breasts lengthways, slightly on the diagonal, into long, very thin slices. Arrange the duck and melon slices on 4 plates and put about 1 tablespoon of the pickled ginger alongside. Sprinkle the dressing around the edge of the plate and serve.

oven-dried tomato and thyme tart

SERVES 8

750 g (1½ lb) vine-ripened
or plum tomatoes
450 g (1 lb) puff pastry
100 g (4 oz) crumbly blue
cheese, such as Blue Vinny,
thinly sliced
1 teaspoon fresh thyme leaves
1 tablespoon olive oil
A handful of wild
rocket leaves
1 tablespoon extra virgin
olive oil
Maldon sea salt flakes and
freshly ground black pepper

1 Preheat the oven to its highest setting. Cut the tomatoes in half lengthways and place them cut-side up in a lightly oiled, shallow roasting tin. Sprinkle over 1½ teaspoons of Maldon salt and some black pepper and roast for 15 minutes. Lower the oven temperature to 150°C/300°F/Gas Mark 2 and roast them for a further 1¼–1½ hours until they have shrivelled in size but are still slightly juicy in the centre. Remove and set aside.

2 Increase the oven temperature to 200°C/400°F/Gas Mark 6. Roll out the pastry on a lightly floured surface into a 30 x 37.5 cm (12 x 15 in) rectangle. Lift it on to a lightly greased baking sheet, prick here and there with a fork and bake blind for 18–20 minutes until crisp and golden. Remove from the oven, carefully turn it over and bake for a further 5 minutes.

3 Arrange the tomatoes haphazardly over the tart base, leaving a narrow border free around the edge. Crumble over the slices of blue cheese, sprinkle over the thyme leaves and drizzle over the olive oil. Return the tart to the oven for 5–6 minutes until the cheese has melted.

4 Remove the tart from the oven and scatter the rocket over the top. Cut it into 8 pieces, sprinkle with the extra virgin olive oil and serve.

SERVES 4

**400 g (14 oz) piece of
unskinned salmon fillet
85 ml (3 fl oz) sunflower oil
Juice of ½ lemon
1 tablespoon chopped dill
2 teaspoons Pernod
1 teaspoon caster sugar
1 teaspoon chopped chives
½ teaspoon salt
and 10 turns of the
black pepper mill**

1 Put 4 plates into the fridge together with the salmon fillet and leave them to get really cold. Shortly before serving, mix all the remaining ingredients together in a bowl.

2 Put the salmon fillet skin-side down on a board. Hold a long, thin-bladed knife at a 45-degree angle and, starting at the tail end of the fillet, cut the salmon into very thin slices. Lay the slices, slightly overlapping, on each chilled plate and spoon over the dressing. Leave for 5 minutes before serving.

TIP

The size of your salmon slices will very much depend on the size of fish your fillet comes from. The larger the fish, the wider the fillet and therefore your slices, but the important thing here is to make sure they are very thin – as thin as smoked salmon if possible. And if the slices come away a bit ragged, don't worry, they will look all right once they are on the plate and covered with the dressing.

crab with rocket, basil and olive oil

350 g (12 oz) fresh white crab meat
2 teaspoons lemon juice
4 teaspoons extra virgin olive oil, flavoured with lemon if possible, plus extra for drizzling
8 basil leaves, finely shredded
A handful of wild rocket leaves
Salt and freshly ground black pepper
Maldon sea salt and cracked black pepper, to garnish

1 Put the crab meat into a bowl and gently stir in the lemon juice, olive oil, basil and some seasoning to taste.

2 Make a small, tall pile of the crab mixture on 4 plates, placing them slightly off centre. Put a small pile of rocket leaves alongside. Drizzle a little more olive oil over the rocket and around the outside edge of the plate, sprinkle the oil with a little sea salt and cracked black pepper and serve.

TIP

Fresh white crab meat is available from most good fishmongers, especially if you give him or her a bit of advance warning. It is also sometimes available pasteurised. Just don't bother to buy dressed crab in the shell because it usually consists of lots of brown meat, which you don't need for this dish, and very little white and is not good value for money either.

grilled tuna salad with guacamole

grilled tuna salad with guacamole

SERVES 4

**450 g (1 lb) long thin piece
of tuna loin fillet (see tip)**
Oil, for brushing
**Salt and coarsely crushed
black pepper**
**Coriander sprigs and lime
wedges, to garnish**

FOR THE GUACAMOLE
1 large avocado
**1 green chilli, seeded
and chopped**
Juice of 1 lime
2 spring onions, chopped
**1 tablespoon
chopped coriander**
1–2 tablespoons sunflower oil

FOR THE SOY DRESSING
1 tablespoon dark soy sauce
1 spring onion, finely chopped
**¼ green Dutch chilli, seeded
and chopped**
Juice and grated zest of ½ lime
**1 teaspoon each finely chopped
lemongrass and fresh ginger**

1 Wrap the piece of tuna tightly in clingfilm so that it looks like a fat sausage. Chill for at least 3 hours, or overnight.

2 Heat a ridged cast-iron griddle until very hot. Unwrap the tuna, brush with oil, sprinkle liberally with salt and crushed pepper and cook for 1–1½ minutes on each face, until coloured all over and cooked to a depth of about 5 mm (¼ in). Remember that the centre of the tuna should remain raw. Remove from the pan, season again and leave to cool.

3 For the guacamole, halve, peel and stone the avocado, crush the flesh into a coarse paste with a fork and stir in the remaining ingredients with ½ teaspoon of salt. Mix the ingredients for the soy dressing together with 1 tablespoon of water.

4 Cut the tuna into thin slices and arrange on 4 plates. Put some guacamole to the side and spoon some of the dressing over the fish. Garnish with the coriander and lime wedges.

TIP
To get the right shape and thickness of tuna for this dish, you ideally need to buy a 20 cm (8 in) long piece of loin, cut from the thicker end of the fillet. Then cut it lengthways into 3 long, narrow pieces. The remaining 2 pieces can be frozen for later use. Alternatively, buy 450 g (1 lb) of thick tuna loin steaks, sear, then carve across into long, thin slices. It won't be identical to the picture but will taste just as good.

sautéed red mullet with spaghettini

SERVES 4

4 small red mullet, weighing
about 150 g (5 oz) each,
filleted (see page 41)
450 g (1 lb) spaghettini
4 tablespoons olive oil
2 garlic cloves, finely chopped
1 medium-hot red chilli,
seeded and
finely chopped
4 plum tomatoes, skinned,
seeded and chopped
20 g (¾ oz) flat-leaf
parsley, finely chopped
Salt and freshly ground
black pepper
Extra virgin olive oil, to serve

1 Cut the mullet fillets across into strips 2 cm (¾ in) wide. Bring 3.4 litres (6 pints) of water to the boil in a large pan with 2 tablespoons of salt. Add the pasta, bring back to the boil and cook for 5 minutes or until *al dente*.

2 Meanwhile, heat the olive oil in a large frying pan. Fry the strips of red mullet, skin-side down, for 3 minutes. Turn them over, fry for 1 minute and then season with salt and pepper.

3 Drain the pasta well and tip it into a large warmed serving bowl. Add the garlic and red chilli to the frying pan with the red mullet and fry for 30 seconds. Add the tomatoes and fry for a further 30 seconds. Tip everything into the bowl with the pasta, scraping up all the little bits that may have stuck to the bottom of the pan, then add 3 tablespoons of the parsley and gently toss everything together so that the fish just begins to break up. Serve immediately, drizzled with extra virgin olive oil and sprinkled with the remaining parsley.

**removing the meat from
a cooked lobster**

1 Twist off the larger claw arms and the legs. Cut away any bands binding the claws together. Break the claw arms apart at the joints and then crack the shell with the back of a knife blade or a hammer.

3 Now cut the lobster in half lengthways. Lift out the intestinal tract which runs down the centre of the meat, then remove the meat from the tail section.

2 Remove the meat from each section of the claws in as large pieces as possible.

5 If you wish to remove the tail meat in one piece for slicing into discs, don't cut the lobster in half lengthways; instead, detach the head from the tail and then cut the head in half and remove the tomalley and roe. Turn the tail section over and cut along either side of the flat under-shell with scissors. Lift back the flap and take out the meat. Slice as required and remove the intestinal tract from each slice with the point of a sharp knife.

4 Remove the soft, greenish tomalley (liver) and any red roe from the head and tail (these are edible).

cleaning mussels

2 Discard any open mussels that do not close when lightly tapped on the work surface. Pull out the tough, fibrous beards protruding from the tightly closed shells.

1 Wash the mussels in plenty of cold water and scrub the shells with a stiff brush. Use a knife to scrape off any barnacles that are sticking to them.

filleting small round fish (such as small sea bass, mackerel, herring and red mullet)

1 Lay the fish on a chopping board with its back towards you. Cut around the back of the head, through the flesh of the fillet down to the backbone, using a sharp, thin-bladed, flexible knife.

2 Turn the knife towards the tail and, beginning just behind the head, carefully start to cut the fillet away from the bones, down towards the belly.

3 Once you have loosened enough flesh to enable you to get the whole blade of the knife underneath the fillet, rest a hand on top of the fish and cut away the fillet in one clean sweep right down to the tail, keeping the blade close to the bones as you do so. Remove any small bones left in the fillet with a pair of tweezers. Turn the fish over and repeat on the other side.

preparing squid

1 Grasp the head in one hand and the body in the other. Gently pull the head and it should come away easily, taking the milky-white intestines with it. You may like to retain the ink sac which will be in the intestines.

3 Reach into the body and pull out the plastic-like quill and the soft white roe, if there is any.

2 Cut the tentacles off the head, then discard the head. Squeeze out the beak-like mouth from the centre of the tentacles, cut it off and discard. The tentacles can either be separated or left intact if very small.

4 Pull off the two fins on either side of the body pouch. Then pull away the purple, semi-transparent skin from both the body and the fins. Wash the pouch out with water. If the pouch is too long and narrow for you to reach right inside when cleaning (and you are not planning to stuff it), a trick for cleaning it out thoroughly is to cut off the very tip and then wash it out with running water, squeezing out any residue as you do so.

Liquid volume measures

1 teaspoon = 5 ml

1 tablespoon (UK/US) = 3 teaspoons = 15 ml

1 tablespoon (AUS) = 4 teaspoons = 20 ml

Note: tablespoon sizes in this book are UK/US, so Australian readers should measure 3 teaspoons where 1 tablespoon is specified in a recipe.

2 fl oz (¼ cup) = 50 ml

4 fl oz (½ cup) = 125 ml

1 cup (8 fl oz) = 250 ml

1 US pint (16 fl oz) = 450 ml

1 UK/AUS pint (20 fl oz) = 600 ml

Cup measures

Cup measurements, which are used by cooks in Australia and America, vary from ingredient to ingredient. You can use kitchen scales to measure solid/dry ingredients, or follow this handy selection of cup measurements for recipes in this book.

bacon/salt pork, diced 100 g (4 oz) = ½ cup

beansprouts 50 g (2 oz) = 1 cup

blue cheese, crumbled or thinly sliced 100 g (4 oz) = 1 cup

butter 25 g (1 oz) = 2 tablespoons (UK/US); 50 g (2 oz) = ¼ cup; 75 g (3 oz) = ⅜ cup

cod, cooked and flaked 450 g (1 lb) = 2 cups

coriander leaves 7 g (¼ oz) = 2 tablespoons

crab meat 350 g (12 oz) = 1½ cups

flour 15 g (½ oz) = 2 tablespoons

ginger, fresh, chopped or sliced 75 g (3 oz) = ½ cup

hazelnuts, whole 20 g (¾ oz) = 2 tablespoons

lobster meat 450–550 g (1–1¼ lb) = 2 cups

parsley, flat-leaf, finely chopped 20 g (¾ oz) = ½ cup

potatoes, peeled and diced 225 g (8 oz) = 1½ cups

rocket leaves, wild 25 g (1 oz) = 1 cup

salt 50 g (2 oz) = ¼ cup

shallot, roughly chopped 7 g (¼ oz) = 1 tablespoon

sugar 25 g (1 oz) = 2 tablespoons; 40 g (1½ oz) = ¼ cup

tomatoes 750 g (1½ lb) = 3 cups

watercress 25 g (1 oz) = 1 cup

Useful equivalents for American and Australian readers

bacon rasher slice of bacon

bacon, streaky, or salt pork sliced bacon

beansprouts mung bean sprouts (*not* alfalfa sprouts)

Blue Vinny a low-fat Dorset blue cheese; substitute other low-fat blue cheese

chilli, red Dutch also known as Holland chilli; substitute fresh, red cayenne pepper or other

chilli, red finger fresh, red cayenne pepper; or substitute Thai pepper or jalapeño pepper

chives if unavailable, substitute green/spring onion tops

coriander (leaves) cilantro or Chinese parsley

cream, double (48% butterfat) whipping or heavy cream

crème fraîche sour cream

curly endive or frisée sometimes called chicory in US, a lacy, bitter-tasting green salad leaf

eggs, medium (UK/AUS) large (US)

flour, plain all-purpose flour

grill broil

groundnut oil peanut oil

Maldon sea salt flakes sea salt (or plain salt)

parsley, flat-leaf Italian parsley

prawns, large tiger prawns or other jumbo shrimp

red mullet substitutes can include orange roughy or sea bass

rocket peppery salad leaf, also known as arugula or roquette

shallots shallot onions (*not* green onions, or spring onions)

Sichuan peppercorns unavailable in US; substitute with Sancho Japanese peppercorns, prickly ash berries or Sichuan pepper oil

spring onions scallions, green onions, or (confusingly in Australia) shallots

sugar, caster a fine-grained sugar; substitute with berry sugar or granulated sugar

water biscuits unsalted crackers

index

The Seafood Restaurant
Riverside
Padstow
Cornwall PL28 8BY

T 01841 532 700
E for table and room bookings:
reservations@rickstein.com

St Petroc's Hotel and Bistro
4 New Street
Padstow
Cornwall PL28 8EA

contact details as for
The Seafood Restaurant

Rick Stein's Café
10 Middle Street
Padstow
Cornwall PL28 8AP

contact details as for
The Seafood Restaurant

Stein's Fish & Chips
Waterfront Business Units
South Quay
Padstow
Cornwall PL28 8BL

contact details as for
The Seafood Restaurant

Stein's Gift Shop
8 Middle Street
Padstow
Cornwall PL28 8AP

T 01841 532 221
F 01841 533 566
E reservations@rickstein.com

Mail order:
T 01841 533 250
F 01841 533 132
E mailorder@rickstein.com

Stein's Patisserie
1 Lanadwell Street
Padstow
Cornwall PL28 8AN

contact details as for
The Seafood Restaurant

Stein's Deli
Waterfront Business Units
South Quay
Padstow
Cornwall PL28 8BL

contact details as for
The Seafood Restaurant

Padstow Seafood School
Waterfront Business Units
South Quay
Padstow
Cornwall PL28 8BL

T 01841 533 466
F 01841 533 344
E seafoodschool@rickstein.com

Website for all information:
www.rickstein.com